The Brain Fitness Workout

Brain training puzzles to improve your
memory, concentration, decision-making
skills and mental flexibility

Philip Carter

KoganPage

LONDON PHILADELPHIA NEW DELHI

Whilst the author has made every effort to ensure that the content of this book is accurate, please note that occasional errors can occur in books of this kind. If you suspect that an error has been made in any of the tests included in this book, please inform the publishers at the address printed below so that it can be corrected at the next reprint.

Publisher's note

Every possible effort has been made to ensure that the information contained in this book is accurate at the time of going to press, and the publishers and author cannot accept responsibility for any errors or omissions, however caused. No responsibility for loss or damage occasioned to any person acting, or refraining from action, as a result of the material in this publication can be accepted by the editor, the publisher or the author.

First published in Great Britain and the United States in 2010 by Kogan Page Limited
Reprinted 2010

120 Pentonville Road	525 South 4th Street, #241	4737/23 Ansari Road
London N1 9JN	Philadelphia PA 19147	Daryaganj
United Kingdom	USA	New Delhi 110002
www.koganpage.com		India

© Philip Carter, 2010

ISBN   978 0 7494 5982 6
E-ISBN   978 0 7494 5983 3

British Library Cataloguing-in-Publication Data

A CIP record for this book is available from the British Library.

Library of Congress Cataloging-in-Publication Data

Carter, Philip.
  The brain fitness workout : brain training puzzles to improve your memory, concentration, decision-making skills and mental flexibility / Philip Carter.
    p. cm.
    ISBN 978-0-7494-5982-6 — ISBN 978-0-7494-5983-3 (ebook)   1. Memory.
2. Decision making.   3. Puzzles.   4. Brain.   I. Title.

  BF370.C37 2010
  153.9′3—dc22

                                                                2010010394

Typeset by Graphicraft Limited, Hong Kong
Production managed by Jellyfish
Printed in the UK by CPI Antony Rowe

Contents

Introduction:
Use it or lose it

We can all utilize our brain potential to a much greater degree, and the use of puzzles and tests is of great value in giving our brain a much needed workout.

Whilst most people are aware of the importance of keeping their bodies in good shape, it is only in recent years that there has been a widespread acceptance that the brain is stimulated by originality, thrives on challenge and needs to be exercised and trained just as much as other parts of the body.

The advantages of exercising the brain are considerable. The brain is the most vital organ of the human body and our most valuable asset. It shapes our speech, skills, thoughts and feelings, yet it has until recently been perhaps a part of our body that we have largely taken for granted and the one that we have tended to neglect the most.

This book includes a wide range of puzzles, tests and workouts designed to provide original and stimulating mental challenges with the aim of improving readers' brain fitness. Several of the exercises are speed tests against the clock, and this is indicated where appropriate. In some cases an assessment rating is provided to enable you to monitor your performance.

Part One and Part Three each consist of an IQ test of approximately the same difficulty level. It is suggested that you tackle the first of these tests at the outset and then tackle the second test after you have attempted a substantial number of the other puzzles and tests, as some improvement in performance on the second test is likely to be noted after you have given your brain a thorough workout.

The range of tests and puzzles includes different sorts of IQ tests, brain-teasers, memory tests and puzzles involving words, numbers and shapes. The variety and scope of the puzzles and tests will stretch and exercise the mind and involve different and, sometimes, original and creative thought processes, many of which will enable us to tackle the real problems of life with renewed vigour and confidence.

Whilst the book is structured to include several different types of brain workouts, the puzzles and tests are also designed to provide fun and entertainment throughout. It is, therefore, up to you how you wish to use the book – either to attempt one workout at a time or simply to dip into the book at random and attempt whichever of the many questions takes your fancy at the time. It is, however, recommended that to derive maximum benefit from the workouts you pace yourself to attempt a number of puzzles each day at a time that is most convenient and when you are feeling least pressured. Also try to vary the type of puzzle you attempt day by day, as different types of puzzle tend to stimulate different types of brain activity.

An analysis of performance on each of the different types of workouts in Part Two is also recommended, as this will enable you to build and capitalize on your strengths, and work even harder on improving performance in any areas of weakness you may have identified.

IQ test

CHAPTER 1

IQ test 1

An IQ (intelligence quotient) test is a standardized test designed to measure human intelligence as distinct from attainments. Intelligence quotient is an age-related measure of intelligence level. The word 'quotient' means the result of dividing one quantity by another, and one definition of intelligence is 'mental ability or quickness of mind'.

Usually, adult IQ tests consist of a graded series of tasks, each of which has been standardized with a large representative population of individuals in order to establish an average IQ of 100 for each test.

There are many different types of IQ tests. However, a typical test might consist of three sections, each testing a different ability, usually verbal reasoning, numerical ability and diagrammatic, or spatial, reasoning. In order to give you the opportunity to practise on all types of questions that you are likely to encounter in actual IQ tests, the two IQ tests that have been specially compiled for this book are multidisciplinary and include a mix of verbal, numerical and diagrammatic questions, as well as additional questions involving logical thought processes and a degree of lateral thinking.

Although it is generally accepted that a person's IQ remains constant throughout life and, therefore, it is not possible to increase your actual IQ, it is possible to improve your performance on IQ tests by practising the many different types of question, and learning to recognize the recurring themes.

As the two IQ tests contained in this book have been newly compiled, they are not therefore standardized, so an actual IQ assessment cannot be given. However, a guide to assessing your performance for each test is provided.

A time limit of 120 minutes is allowed for completion of all 40 questions. The correct answers are given at the end of the test, and you should award yourself one point for each completely correct answer. Calculators should not be used to assist with solving numerical questions. However, written notes may be made.

1 Which number will correctly complete the equation?

| 3 | 4 | × | 1 | 6 | = | 5 | ? | 4 |

| 3 | 4 | 6 | 8 |
| A | B | C | D |

Answer

2 Which two words are most opposite in meaning?
charge, adopt, retire, refuse, reclaim, formulate

Answer

3 The price of a television that has been discounted by 15% is £178.50. What was the original price of the television?

Answer

4 Which word in brackets is most similar in meaning to the word in capitals?
LOPSIDED (unsafe, loquacious, narrow, asymmetrical, pruned)

Answer

5   If A = 2, B = 3, C = 4 and D = 7, solve the equation below.

$$\frac{(A^A + D) \times C}{D + C} \times \frac{B \times C}{A + C}$$

Answer

6   Select two words that are synonyms, plus an antonym of these two synonyms, from the list of words below:
aggressive, intrepid, punitive, insipid, pusillanimous, vacuous, audacious

Answer

7

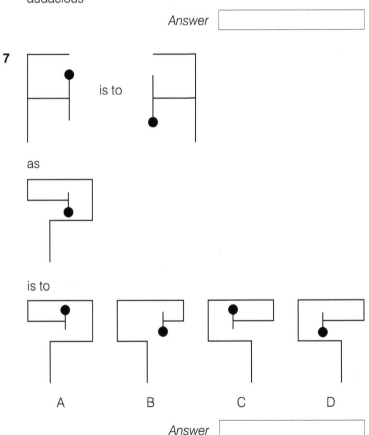

is to

as

is to

| A | B | C | D |

Answer

8   Which two words are closest in meaning?
buttery, largesse, hope, generosity, greatest, distraction

Answer

9 What number should replace the question mark?

Answer

10 Which is the odd one out?
fixed, still, stationery, immobile, motionless

Answer

11 A lorry travels at an average speed of 48 mph for 2 hours. By how much does it have to increase its average speed for it to travel an extra 18 miles in the next two hours?

Answer

12 Identify two words (one from each set of brackets) that form a connection (analogy), thereby relating to the words in capitals in the same way.
LOGIC   (science, pure, reason, system)
INTUITION   (cognition, instinct, knowing, thought)

Answer

13 What number should replace the question mark?

7	9	3	1	9
8	6	2	1	6
9	8	7	2	4
6	9	8	2	3
5	2	?	1	3

Answer

14 Which word in brackets is most similar in meaning to the word in capitals?
PROSAIC (poetical, decent, mundane, augural, imminent)

Answer [   ]

15 What number should replace the question marks?
3682, 46, 7394, 21, 6889, ??

Answer [   ]

16 How many lines appear below?

Answer [   ]

17 Which two words are most opposite in meaning?
worried, outmoded, ordinary, irrational, traditional, noteworthy

Answer [   ]

18 Which two words when combined mean IDYLLIC?
able, oral, host, wise, past, some, hand, acre

Answer [   ]

19 Which two words are closest in meaning?

piety, sacrilege, despondency, profanity, oblation, immunity

Answer [   ]

20

Answer [   ]

21 A market stallholder receives a delivery of eggs but is angry to find that several are cracked. He counts them up and finds that 136 were cracked, which is 16% of the total delivery. How many eggs in total were in the delivery?

Answer [   ]

22 Insert a word in the brackets so that it completes a word or phrase when tacked on to the word on the left and completes another word or phrase when placed in front of the word on the right.

TRAP   (   ) WAY

Answer

23 Work from letter to adjacent letter horizontally and vertically, but not diagonally, to spell out a 12-letter word. You must find the starting point and provide the missing letter.

T	S	S	M
S	E	I	O
I		O	L

Answer

24 Select two words that are synonyms, plus an antonym of these two synonyms, from the list of words below.

denude, depreciate, clothe, reduce, augment, disarrange, discourage

Answer

25

Which is the missing tile?

A   B   C   D   E   F

Answer

26 In each square find the starting point and spiral clockwise to find an eight-letter word. The two words are synonyms. You must provide the missing letters.

L	E	A		E	A	M
				L		I
T	N	A			A	

Answer

27 What is the meaning of EMPYREAL?
A relating to observation or experiment
B celestial
C capable of flight
D majestic
E formal speech

Answer

28

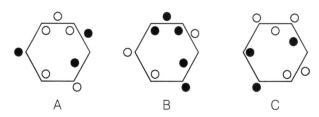

A   B   C

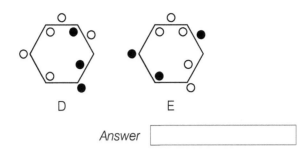

D   E

Answer [   ]

29 In the two numerical sequences below, one number that appears in the top sequence should appear in the bottom sequence and vice versa. Which two numbers should be changed round?

100,   99,   97,   94,   89,   85,   79,   72
105,   104,   101,   96,   90,   80,   69,   56

Answer [   ]

30 What number should replace the question mark?

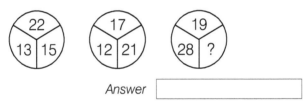

Answer [   ]

31

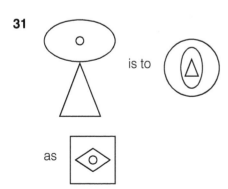

is to (△)

as

is to

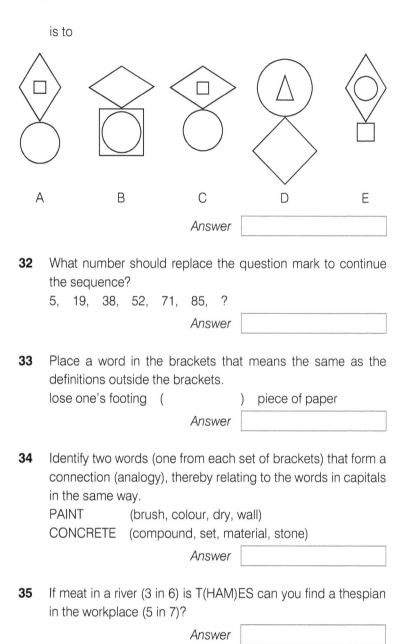

A   B   C   D   E

Answer [   ]

32   What number should replace the question mark to continue
the sequence?
5,   19,   38,   52,   71,   85,   ?

Answer [   ]

33   Place a word in the brackets that means the same as the
definitions outside the brackets.
lose one's footing   (   )   piece of paper

Answer [   ]

34   Identify two words (one from each set of brackets) that form a
connection (analogy), thereby relating to the words in capitals
in the same way.
PAINT   (brush, colour, dry, wall)
CONCRETE   (compound, set, material, stone)

Answer [   ]

35   If meat in a river (3 in 6) is T(HAM)ES can you find a thespian
in the workplace (5 in 7)?

Answer [   ]

36 Place a word in the brackets that means the same as the definitions outside the brackets.

prevaricate   (   ) recline

Answer [   ]

37 What is one-half of one-third of three-quarters of one-quarter of one-quarter of one-quarter of one-third of 384?

Answer [   ]

38

What comes next?

A   B   C   D

Answer [   ]

39 What number should replace the question mark to continue the sequence?

13,   26,   39,   ?,   65

Answer [   ]

40 Change the position of four words only in the sentence below so that it then makes complete sense.

The sidereal time is the day that the stars takes to rotate once relative to the earth.

Answer [   ]

Answers

1 B: 4
2 adopt, refuse
3 £210
4 asymmetrical
5 8: $\dfrac{(2^2+7)\times 4}{7+4}\times\dfrac{3\times 4}{2+4}$
6 Synonyms: intrepid, audacious
Antonym: pusillanimous
7 C: the figure is a mirror image and the line with the dot flips horizontally
8 largesse, generosity
9 24: (5 + 3) × 3
10 stationery: it means writing materials; the rest mean stationary
11 9 mph
96 miles in 2 hours = 48 mph
114 miles in 2 hours = 57 mph
12 reason, instinct
13 6: 5 + 2 + 6 = 13
14 mundane
15 21: 89 − 68
16 14
17 ordinary, noteworthy
18 past and oral = pastoral
19 sacrilege, profanity
20 A: the whole figure rotates 90° anticlockwise and the two squares change places
21 850: (136 ÷ 16) × 100
22 door

23 seismologist
24 Synonyms: depreciate, reduce
Antonym: augment
25 D: looking across and down, each row and column contains
one each of three different size circles, and also one circle with
a line and one with a dot
26 pleasant, amicable
27 B
28 E: dots move from the outside to inside and vice versa and
change from black to white and vice versa.
29 89 and 90 should be swapped round.
The top sequence progresses −1, −2, −3, −4, −5, −6, −7.
The bottom sequence progresses −1, −3, −5, −7, −9, −11,
−13.
30 3: the numbers in each circle total 50
31 A: The first analogy is being reversed. The diamond increases
in size and goes at the top, the square reduces in size and
goes inside the diamond, and the circle increases in size and
goes to the bottom of the diamond.
32 104: add 14 and 19 respectively
33 slip
34 dry, set
35 f(actor)y
36 lie
37 1
38 A: each of the three rectangles within the box is moving down
one place at a time in turn.
39 52: add 13 each time
40 The sidereal **day** is the **time** that the **earth** takes to rotate
once relative to the **stars**.

Assessment

Score 1 point for each correct answer.

Total score	Rating	Percentage of population
37–40	Genius level	Top 5%
32–36	High expert	Top 10%
28–31	Expert	Top 30%
24–27	High average	Top 40%
17–23	Middle average	Top 60%
13–16	Low average	Bottom 40%
9–12	Borderline low	Bottom 30%
5–8	Low	Bottom 10%
0–4	Very low	Bottom 5%

PART TWO

The workouts

CHAPTER 2

Keenness of mind

Keenness, or agility, of mind is the ability to think quickly and react instinctively. It is a valuable asset to have at one's disposal in many situations.

All the tests in this chapter are speed tests, where it is necessary to keep calm and maintain your concentration whilst working against the clock. Agility of mind tests when set against the clock are an ideal tool for exercising and sharpening up the mind. In themselves the questions are not particularly difficult. However, when they are presented as a series to be attempted within a set time limit, the brain must adapt to the situation before it, and agility of mind, plus a high degree of concentration, is required in order to score highly.

Speed exercise

In this 20-question speed test it is necessary to maintain your concentration whilst working against the clock. The test contains an eclectic mixture of verbal, mathematical, logical and lateral thinking questions.

It is recommended that any numerical questions are solved without the use of a calculator in order to derive maximum benefit.

You have 45 minutes in which to answer the 20 questions.

1 Write the word IDEA in reverse under the word TOWN and write the word CALM in reverse above the word TIME but below the word IDEA. What word appears reading down the right-hand column?

Answer

2 Arrange the letters in forward alphabetic order followed by the numbers in descending order.

T S 4 9 2 K L Z N 8 H 7 P

Answer

3 What is 70% of 550?

Answer

4 How many times does this sentence contain the letter t?

Answer

5 In the English alphabet, which letter comes two letters before the letter that comes six letters after the letter M?

Answer

6 Place the following words into alphabetical order:
abiding, abashes, abdomen, abettor, abating, ability, abalone, abature, abandon, abactor, abators

Answer

7 When full, a barrel of water contains 75 litres. How many litres remain after 45% has been used?

Answer

8 Which is the greater, 56 × 3 or 85% of 200?

Answer

9 What letter should replace the question mark?

? M U A N Y E

Answer

10 What word should replace the question mark?

TEA, SEA, ?, SOT, HOT

Answer

11 What letter comes next?

A B D C E F H G I J ?

Answer

12 What day and date comes exactly 38 days after Thursday 25 June?

Answer

13 What number should replace the question mark to continue the sequence?

1, 3, 7, 9, 13, ?

Answer

14 ADORE AGENT is an anagram of which two types of fruit?

Answer

15 What comes next?

calm, able, brim, rock

A care   B omit   C ring   D edit   E unto

Answer

16 In the phrase below the first letter of each word has been removed, as well as spacing. What is the phrase?

A R D O I N D

Answer

17 The letters that are in the wrong alphabetical order in the list below can be rearranged to spell out which six-letter word?

L B C D E F G H P J K A M N O I Q S R T U V W X Y Z

Answer [   ]

18 What comes next in the sequence below?

542, 538, 535, 532, 529, ???

Answer [   ]

19 BOIL TAR is an anagram of which seven-letter word?

Answer [   ]

20 Split the list of numbers into two parts, so that each part adds up to the same total. Do not change the order in which the numbers appear in the list.

5 9 7 3 2 6 1 4 6 9 7 1 6

Answer [   ]

Answers

1 NICE:
TOW**N**
AED**I**
MLA**C**
TIM**E**

2 H K L N P S T Z 9 8 7 4 2

3 385

4 8

5 Q

6 abactor, abalone, abandon, abashes, abating, abators, abature, abdomen, abettor, abiding, ability

7 41.25

8 85% of 200 (170). 56 × 3 = 168

9 J: alternate letters spell JUNE and MAY

10 SET: TEA is being changed to HOT, one letter at a time

11 L: every third and fourth letter of the alphabet are being reversed

12 Sunday 2 August

13 15: add 2 and 4 alternately

14 orange, date

15 B. omit: each word commences with the second letter of the previous word

16 hard to find

17 spiral

18 527: deduct the value of the middle digit at each stage, eg $542 - 4 = 538$

19 orbital

20 5 9 7 3 2 6 1 and 4 6 9 7 1 6
Both parts = 33

Assessment

Score 1 point for each correct answer.

18–20	Exceptional
16–17	Very good
12–15	Good
8–11	Average

Repeated symbols exercise

In each of the following 15 questions, identify the symbol that appears the most and enter the number of times it appears, together with a sketch of the symbol in the box provided.

For example:

☺ ○ ♣☺ ♪♦♣♪♀ ♫♪♣♥ ☺ ♪╪↕∏↕♪♣♀

Answer ☐ ☐

Answer ♪ 5

The symbol that appears most times is ♪ and it appears in the list five times.

This is a speed test against the clock. You have a target time of 20 minutes in which to complete the 15 questions.

1 ╫ ® § ¢ ∑ ↕ £ ¢ ♪ £ ↕ ╫ ¢ ● ☼ ∑ $ ●

Answer ☐ ☐

2 ♥ ☺ ♂ ♫ ╫ § ☺ ♣ ♦ ☼ ♥ ♪ ▲ ╫ ∏ ╫ ●♦♪ ♣ ∂ € ♦ ≠

Answer ☐ ☐

3 $ @ ♫ ╫ ▲ ♪ € ♪ $ & $ & ♪♫&♦↕ ♫ ╫ ¥ ♪ ▲ ╫ @ ∂

Answer ☐ ☐

4 ╥ ╚╝ ╢╡ ╤ ╧ ╫ ╝ ‖ ╞╩ ╫ ╁ ╛ ╧ ╕

Answer ☐ ☐

5 ▌ ▪ ◀▄ ♥ ▣ ●♥ — ◥ ▄ ▣ ◀● ◀▪● ▌ ◥ ● ▣

Answer ☐ ☐

6 ■ ▐ ▪ — ▲ ▶ ● ▫ ▣ ♠ ♣ ♥ ♦ ♫ ▪ ▐█ ▓ ♀

Answer ☐ ☐

7] @ ¡ ¢ £ ¤ ¥ § © ® ¿] ¡ ¢ £ ¤ ¥ §] ¿ ® ©

Answer ☐ ☐

8 π ξ £ ¥ ♀ @ ¢ § ¿ ¤ π ∑ Ω Θ ¶ ® $ % ! { }

Answer ☐ ☐

9 ¶ § © « ® ¥ £ ¢ § « ¥ ¢ £ § « ¶ ® ¥ § ¢ © ¶ $ £ ¶ ® § ∑

Answer ☐ ☐

10 ¡ ¢ £ ¤ ¥ § © « ® ± µ ¶ ¿ ¡ Θ Ω X Ξ π £ € ∞

Answer ☐ ☐

11 ┼ ‖ ┏┑ ┑ ┑ ┕┑ ┕╫ ┴ ┕┕┑ ‖ ┴╫ ┏┤┤ ┠

Answer ☐ ☐

12 ◀ ▌▐ ▓ ▪ ▶ ■ ▼ ▲ ▪ ◀ — ▌◙ ▓ ◀ ▼ ■ ▲ —

Answer ☐ ☐

13 & $ @ ? } ¢ ¥ § © ® ¶ Ω £ } ¢ ? ¥ @ § # ® # ¶ $ Ω ¢ £

Answer ☐ ☐

14 ₪ € ‰ † Ω e ↕ → ↔ † ₪ → € ‰ Ω ↕ → e ↔ e ↕ → ↔ Ω † ‰ € ₪

Answer ☐ ☐

15 ◻△∩ ∟ ◻ ○ ♂ ∩ ◇ △ ◻ ∟ ♂ ○ ∟ ∩ → ◇ ∟ △ ♂ ◇ ○ ◻ ♂ ₪ → ○ ◻ ◇ △ ∟ ∩ ♂ ○ ◻ ∟ ∩ △ ◇ → ₪ ♂ ₪ ○ → ◻ ◇ ∟ △ ∩

Answer ☐ ☐

Answers

1	¢	3		**9**	§	5
2	♦	3		**10**	¡	2
3	♪	4		**11**	┖	3
4	⊥	2		**12**	◀	3
5	●	4		**13**	¢	3
6	■	2		**14**	→	4
7	]	3		**15**	∟	7
8	π	2				

Assessment

15	Superb
13–14	Excellent
11–12	Good
9–10	Above average
7–8	Average
5–6	Below average
0–4	Weak

Letter/code change exercise

Target time: 45 minutes

Section 1

Code	Function
♫	Exchange the second and fourth letters
Σ	Delete the seventh letter
&	Add the letter X between the third and fourth letters
¶	Reverse the whole sequence
◄	Reverse the last three letters
Ω	Add the letters PJ to the end of the sequence

Example

T N Y D F C W Z

→   ♫ + & + ¶

Answer | Z W C F N X Y D T |

Explanation

Stage 1: ♩ Exchange the letters N and D = T D Y N F C W Z

Stage 2: & Add the letter X between the third and fourth letters =
TD Y X N F C W Z

Stage 3: ¶ Reverse the whole sequence = Z W C F N X Y D T

1 Z K L D F N A T
→ ◀ + ¶ + ♩

Answer

2 J Y E B Z G A P K
→ Σ + Ω + &

Answer

3 X N J E O L K D S T
→ ♩ + Ω + ¶

Answer

4 N D K L M J B X T V R P
→ ◀ + Σ + ¶

Answer

5 Z X C V B N M L K J H
→ Σ + ♩ + Ω + ¶

Answer

6 P O I U Y T R E W Q
→ ◀ + ¶ + & + ◀

Answer

7 L K J H G F D S A Z X
→ ¶ + Σ + ♩ + ◀ + Ω

Answer

8 I O P J K L B N M Q A Z
→ Σ + Ω + & + ♫ + ◄ + Ω

Answer [   ]

9 T R E N O P Z L X Y F W
→ Ω + ♫ + ◄ + Σ + & + Ω + ¶

Answer [   ]

10 Z N D L F A M E K F M S Y
→ ◄ + ¶ + ♫ + Ω + Σ + & + ♫ + &

Answer [   ]

Section 2: double letter/code change exercise

Code	Function
♫	Exchange the second letter of the top row with the last letter of the bottom row
►	Advance the fourth letter of the bottom row by two places in the alphabet
☺	Add the letter W between the fourth and fifth letters of the top row
╬	Reverse the whole of the bottom row
♪	Reverse the first three letters of the top row
Σ	Exchange the first and last letters of the bottom row

Example

G M K T A P M
J S D A B T U L
→ ╬ + ► + ♪

Answer
K M G T A P M
L U T D A D S J

Explanation

Stage 1 ╬ Reverse the whole of the bottom row
G M K T A P M
L U T B A D S J

Stage 2 ► Advance the fourth letter of the bottom row by two
places in the alphabet

G M K T A P M
L U T D A D S J

Stage 3 ♪ Reverse the first three letters of the top row

K M G T A P M
L U T D A D S J

11 B U T T E R B U R
C O L T S F O O T
→ ☺ + ♪ + ►

Answer

12 C A L O S T O M A
L U T E S C E N S
→ ♯ + Σ + ♫

Answer

13 F A C S I M I L E
T E L E G R A P H
→ ♯ + ☺ + ♫

Answer

14 N E W T O N I A N
M E C H A N I C S
→ ♪ + ♫ + ♯

Answer

15 C R O T A L E R I A
S A G I T A L L I S
→ ♪ + ♯ + ♫ + ☺

Answer

16 P U N C T U A T E D
E Q U I L I B R I A
→ ‖ + ♫ + Σ + ☺ + ♪

Answer

17 E S E M P L A S T I C
I M A G I N A T I O N
→ ♫ + Σ + ☺ + ▶ + ‖

Answer

18 S U B T R O P I C A L
A N T I C Y C L O N E
→ ▶ + ‖ + ♫ + Σ + ‖ + ☺

Answer

19 D I S J U N C T I V E
C O N J U N C T I O N
→ ▶ + Σ + ♫ + ‖ + ♪ + ▶ + ☺

Answer

20 E X P E R I M E N T A L
V E R I F I C A T I O N
→ ‖ + Σ + ♫ + ☺ + ♪ + Σ + ♫

Answer

Answers

1 N F T A D L K Z
2 J Y E X B Z G P K P J
3 J P T S D K L O N J E X

4 VRPTXJMLKDN
5 JPHJKLNBXCVZ
6 EWQXRTYUPOI
7 XSAZDFHLKJPJ
8 IXPOJKLNMQAJPZPJ
9 JPWPJFYXLPORXENT
10 MXYXFSKEAFLDNZPJ
11 TUBTWERBUR
   COLVSFOOT
12 CSLOSTOMA
   LNECSETUA
13 FTCSWIMILE
   HPARGELEA
14 WSNTONIAN
   ECINAHCEM
15 OSCTWALERIA
   SILLATIGAR
16 NEPCWTUATED
   UIRBILIUQA
17 ENEMWPLASTIC
   IOITANIIAMS
18 SABTWROPICAL
   ENTKCYCLONU
19 SCDJWUNCTIVE
   IOIVCNULNON
20 PVEEWRIMENTAL
   XOITACIFIREN

Assessment

Score 1 point for each correct answer.

18–20	Exceptional
16–17	Very good
12–15	Good
8–11	Average

Find the letter exercise

Find nine letters by following the nine sets of instructions and then rearrange the nine letters to spell out a nine-letter word in the English language. Time limit: 30 minutes.

A	B	C	D	E	F	G	H

1 Which letter is three to the left of the letter that is five to the right of the letter immediately to the left of the letter C?

Answer

2 Which letter is two to the right of the letter that is immediately to the left of the letter four to the right of the letter C?

Answer

3 Which letter is three to the right of the letter that is midway between the letter immediately to the left of the letter B and the letter three to the left of the letter F?

Answer

4 Which letter is twice as many places to the right of the letter D as the letter C is to the left of the letter E?

Answer

5 Which letter is three to the left of the letter two to the right of the letter four to the left of the letter immediately to the right of the letter E?

Answer

6 Which letter is immediately to the left of the letter four to the left of the letter that is midway between the letter immediately to the right of the letter G and the letter three to the right of the letter A?

Answer

7 Which letter is half as many places to the left of the letter immediately to the left of the letter F as the letter A is away from the letter two places to the right of the letter E?

Answer

8 Which letter is midway between the letter immediately to the left of the letter C and the letter two to the right of the letter F?

Answer

9 Which letter is three places to the left of the letter that is immediately to the right of the letter that is three to the right of the letter immediately to the left of the letter C?

Answer

Nine-letter word

Answers

1	D		**6**	A
2	H		**7**	B
3	E		**8**	E
4	H		**9**	C
5	A			

Nine-letter-word: BEACHHEAD

Assessment

Award yourself 1 point for each correct answer plus 3 bonus points for the anagram. A total of 12 points are, therefore, available.

12	Excellent
7–9	Very good
5–6	Good
4	Average
2–3	Below average
0–1	Weak

Word/symbol speed exercise

In each question find the longest word that is spelled out by substituting letters for symbols in accordance with the key below.

Example

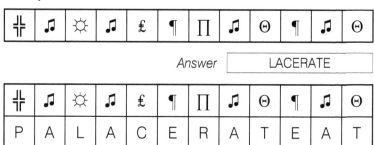

Answer | LACERATE

The words PAL, PALACE, LACE, ACE, ACER, ERA, RAT, RATE, ATE, TEA, EAT, AT and TEAT also appear, but LACERATE is the longest word that appears.

Now try the following. A target time limit of 20 minutes is suggested for the completion of all 10 questions.

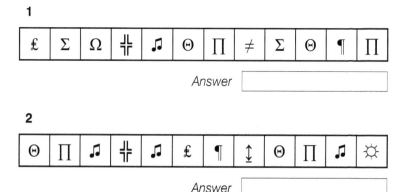

1

Answer

2

Answer

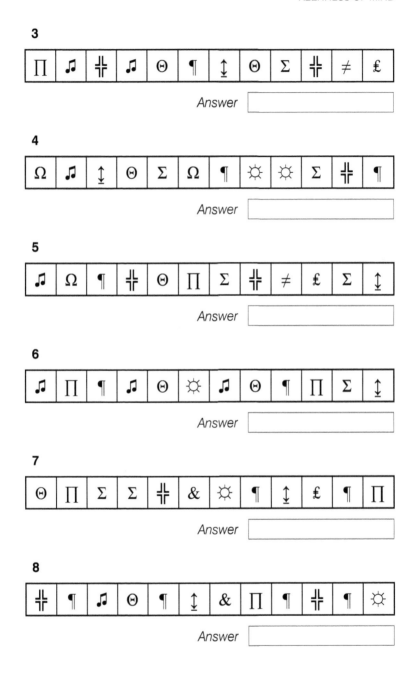

3

| Π | ♫ | ‡ | ♫ | Θ | ¶ | ↕ | Θ | Σ | ‡ | ≠ | £ |

Answer

4

| Ω | ♫ | ↕ | Θ | Σ | Ω | ¶ | ☼ | ☼ | Σ | ‡ | ¶ |

Answer

5

| ♫ | Ω | ¶ | ‡ | Θ | Π | Σ | ‡ | ≠ | £ | Σ | ↕ |

Answer

6

| ♫ | Π | ¶ | ♫ | Θ | ☼ | ♫ | Θ | ¶ | Π | Σ | ↕ |

Answer

7

| Θ | Π | Σ | Σ | ‡ | & | ☼ | ¶ | ↕ | £ | ¶ | Π |

Answer

8

| ‡ | ¶ | ♫ | Θ | ¶ | ↕ | & | Π | ¶ | ‡ | ¶ | ☼ |

Answer

9

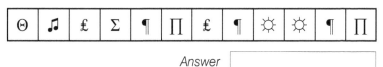

Answer

10

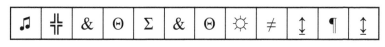

Answer

Answers

1	PATRIOT	6	LATER
2	CENTRAL	7	OPULENCE
3	PATENT	8	TENURE
4	TOWEL	9	COERCE
5	TROPIC	10	OUTLINE

Fours

Fit all the four-letter words listed below into the grid to complete the crossword. Target time: 30 minutes.

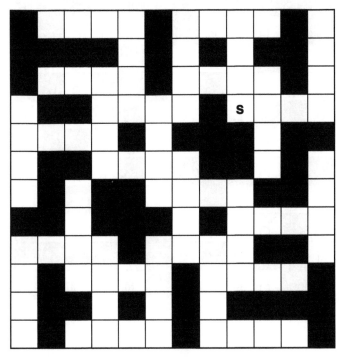

YELP ATOM TIME POLO SKIP AXIS OATH COSY EPIC ANON
NOUN TIDE IRIS NEAR SOAP GRIP AUNT OUST NEWT NOSE
SHOW YAWN KNIT EARN HOST AKIN ONCE GALA STEM
MIST NUMB ONTO

Answer

	N¹	O	U²	N		S³	K⁴	I	P		Y⁵
			E			T		R			E
	S⁶	H	O⁷	W		E⁸	P	I	C⁹		L
Y¹⁰			A¹¹	T¹²	O	M		S¹³	O	A	P
A¹⁴	U	N	T		U			S			
W			H¹⁵	O	S	T¹⁶		Y			M¹⁷
N		P¹⁸			T¹⁹	I	D	E²⁰			I
		O				M		A²¹	X	I	S
G²²	A	L²³	A		N²⁴	E	A²⁵	R			T
R		O²⁶	N	T	O		K²⁷	N	I	T	
I			O		S		I				
P		O²⁸	N	C	E		N²⁹	U	M	B	

Numerical ability

We all require some numerical skills in our lives, whether it is to calculate our weekly shopping bill or to budget how to use our monthly income. The numerical ability exercises in this chapter are designed to strengthen your capacity to perform basic arithmetic functions and encourage you to think numerically. The strengthening of your numerical prowess can also assist you in other areas of life, as many everyday tasks require arithmetical operations or thought processes even though numbers may not be involved.

Addition and multiplication exercises

Complete the addition table by adding the numbers along the top to the numbers down the side. For example, referring to the numbers already inserted in the addition exercise, 7 + 15 = 22, 37 + 6 = 43 and 14 + 9 = 23.

In the multiplication exercise, complete the table by multiplying the numbers along the top with the numbers down the side in accordance with the example already inserted, 8 × 6 = 48.

Try to complete the exercise in your head without the use of a calculator. However, pencil and paper can be used to make notes.

Target time: 10 minutes for the addition exercise and 15 minutes for the multiplication exercise.

Addition exercise

+	9	15	6	27
8				
13				
7		22		
19				
26				
37			43	
14	23			
54				

Multiplication exercise

×	4	9	6	12	8
7					
13					
8			48		
11					
9					
15					
14					
25					
32					

Answers

Addition exercise

+	9	15	6	27
8	17	23	14	35
13	22	28	19	40
7	16	22	13	34
19	28	34	25	46
26	35	41	32	53
37	46	52	43	64
14	23	29	20	41
54	63	69	60	81

Multiplication exercise

×	4	9	6	12	8
7	28	63	42	84	56
13	52	117	78	156	104
8	32	72	48	96	64
11	44	99	66	132	88
9	36	81	54	108	72
15	60	135	90	180	120
14	56	126	84	168	112
25	100	225	150	300	200
32	128	288	192	384	256

Numerical equation speed exercise

This exercise requires you to work quickly and accurately against the clock to extract information from a grid and then apply your powers of mental arithmetic to arrive at the correct answer.

	A	B	C	D	E
P	9	4	8	6	5
Q	7	5	6	4	2
R	6	9	3	8	4
S	7	2	5	8	3
T	3	2	9	7	5

Each number is represented by a pair of letters, for example PC = 8, TD = 7 and, therefore, PCTD = 87.

Examples
SD + CR = 8 + 3 = 11
SDCR × TD = 83 × 7 = 581
(SC × DR) + RE = (5 × 8) + 4 = 44

You are allowed 60 minutes in which to solve the 20 questions below. It is recommended that this exercise is attempted without the use of a calculator in order to derive maximum benefit.

1 QD + CT

Answer [ ]

2 $\dfrac{CR}{SA} \times REBR$

Answer [ ]

3 (ET × QACR) + EQDS

Answer [   ]

4 TBRD × QC

Answer [   ]

5 (CS × QABR) − RCDS

Answer [   ]

6 $\dfrac{AQQB}{EP}$

Answer [   ]

7 (RCBS × CTQE) + RBPD

Answer [   ]

8 (AR + PBES) × (DQ + QCCT)

Answer [   ]

9 $\dfrac{ES}{DR} \times DTQE$

Answer [   ]

10 $\dfrac{RCEP - BSTA}{ES}$

Answer [   ]

11 $\dfrac{RBER \times RE}{TB}$

Answer [   ]

12 $\dfrac{TC}{QEAS} \times AQQE$

Answer [   ]

13 (RADS − QDDT) × PBCR

Answer [   ]

14 (DR + RBTB) − (SDBQ − TC)

Answer [   ]

15 $(DP \times TBSD) - \dfrac{(DR)}{(RE)}$

Answer

16 PCARCT + ESCRBQ

Answer

17 $\dfrac{DTREAQ}{PA}$

Answer

18 $\dfrac{PBCRET}{SBRB}$

Answer

19 (SACRES − TD) × EQSB

Answer

20 PCDSETQA − ARTDCRRE

Answer

Answers

1 4 + 9 = 13

2 $\dfrac{3}{7} \times 49 = 21$

3 (5 × 73) + 28 = 393

4 28 × 6 = 168

5 (5 × 79) − 38 = 357

6 $\dfrac{75}{5} = 15$

7 (32 × 92) + 96 = 3,040

8 (6 + 43) × (4 + 69) = 3,577

9 $\dfrac{3}{8} \times 72 = 27$

10 $\dfrac{35 - 23}{3} = 4$

11 $\dfrac{94}{2} \times 4 = 188$

12 $\dfrac{9}{27} \times 72 = 24$

13 $(68 - 47) \times 43 = 903$

14 $(8 + 92) - (85 - 9) = 24$

15 $(6 \times 28) - \dfrac{8}{4} = 166$

16 $869 + 335 = 1{,}204$

17 $\dfrac{747}{9} = 83$

18 $\dfrac{435}{29} = 15$

19 $(733 - 7) \times 22 = 15{,}972$

20 $8{,}857 - 6{,}734 = 2{,}123$

Assessment

Score 1 point for each correct answer.

18–20	Exceptional
16–17	Very good
12–15	Good
8–11	Average

Progressive numerical matrix exercise

In each question an incomplete matrix of numbers is displayed. In each puzzle all the lines across have a certain mathematical progression. Similarly, all the lines down have a certain mathematical progression. From the information provided you have to decide, by looking across each line and down each column, what mathematical progressions are occurring and fill in all the remaining numbers. In each case there is sufficient information provided to establish what pattern or sequence is occurring, looking at lines both across and down.

Allow yourself a target time of 45 minutes in which to complete the six questions. It is recommended that this exercise is attempted without the use of a calculator in order to derive maximum benefit.

Example

6	10	13
8	12	15
7	11	14

Lines across progress +4, +3. Lines down progress +2, −1.

1

3		6	9
	6	8	
9			15
	16		

2

	9		15
3	7		
		16	
	12	14	

3

		12	
	12		24
		18	72
2		3	

4

	28		32
6			25
	34		
	27	16	

5

4				
		12	17	
1			8	
14	22			14
		8		

6

		23		21	
17	30		19		
			12		18
		31			21
		48	32		
				37	

Answers

1

3	4	6	9
5	6	8	11
9	10	12	15
15	16	18	21

Lines across progress +1, +2, +3. Lines down progress +2, +4, +6.

2

5	9	11	15
3	7	9	13
10	14	16	20
8	12	14	18

Lines across progress +4, +2, +4. Lines down progress −2, +7, −2.

3

8	24	12	48
4	12	6	24
12	36	18	72
2	6	3	12

Lines across progress ×3, ÷2, ×4. Lines down progress ÷2, ×3, ÷6.

4

13	28	17	32
6	21	10	25
19	34	23	38
12	27	16	31

Lines across progress +15, −11, +15. Lines down progress −7, +13, −7.

5

4	12	6	11	4
10	18	12	17	10
1	9	3	8	1
14	22	16	21	14
6	14	8	13	6

Lines across progress +8, −6, +5, −7. Lines down progress +6, −9, +13, −8.

6

5	18	23	7	21	13
17	30	35	19	33	25
10	23	28	12	26	18
13	26	31	15	29	21
30	43	48	32	46	38
21	34	39	23	37	29

Lines across progress +13, +5, −16, +14, −8. Lines down progress +12, −7, +3, +17, −9.

Double number sequence exercise

In order to correctly solve a numerical sequence puzzle it is necessary to identify a pattern of progression that is occurring in the sequence. The numbers in the sequence may be increasing, or they may be decreasing, and in some cases they may be both increasing and decreasing within the sequence. It is up to you to determine how any particular sequence is progressing.

For example, in the following sequence:

1, 9, 17, 25, 33, ?

the missing number is 41, as the numbers in the sequence are increasing by 8 each time.

However, in the more complex sequence:

100, 99, 97, 96, 94, 93, ?

the missing number is 91, as the numbers in the sequence are decreasing by 1 and 2 alternately.

In each of the following questions, in the two numerical sequences given, one number that appears in the top sequence should appear in the bottom sequence and vice versa. Which two numbers should be changed round in each question to make each sequence follow a regular pattern?

It is recommended that this exercise is attempted without the use of a calculator in order to derive maximum benefit.

You have 60 minutes in which to answer the 10 questions.

1   7, 8, 10, 11, 12, 14, 16, 17, 19
9, 11, 10, 13, 11, 13, 12, 14, 13

Answer

2   100, 97, 91, 87, 82, 79, 73
90, 94, 88, 91, 84, 88, 81

Answer

3   10, 14, 11, 15, 11, 16, 13
20, 13, 18, 12, 16, 9, 14

Answer

4   17, 20, 24, 27, 35, 42, 50
21, 22, 26, 29, 31, 32, 36

Answer

5   20, 25, 32, 41, 48, 65, 80
15, 24, 35, 52, 63, 80, 99

Answer

6 1,000, 948, 1,006, 954, 1,135, 960, 1,018
1,200, 1,130, 1,205, 1,012, 1,210, 1,140, 1,215

Answer [   ]

7 2, 5, 11, 28, 47, 95
2, 4, 10, 23, 82, 244

Answer [   ]

8 17, 34, 51, 68, 85, 108
18, 36, 54, 72, 90, 102

Answer [   ]

9 15, 17, 21, 27, 35, 47, 57
12, 15, 20, 27, 36, 45, 60

Answer [   ]

10 6, 12, 13, 26, 28, 56, 53
8, 16, 15, 30, 28, 56, 59

Answer [   ]

Answers

1 12 and 13 should be swapped round. The top sequence progresses: +1, +2, etc. The bottom sequence progresses: +2, −1, etc.

2 87 and 88 should be swapped round. The top sequence progresses: −3, −6, etc. The bottom sequence progresses: +4, −7, etc.

3 11 and 12 should be swapped round. The top sequence progresses: +4, −3, etc. The bottom sequence progresses: −7, +5, etc.

4 27 and 29 should be swapped round. The top sequence progresses: +3, +4, +5, +6, +7, +8. The bottom sequence progresses: +1, +4, etc.

5 48 and 52 should be swapped round. The top sequence progresses: +5, +7, +9, +11, +13, +15. The bottom sequence progresses: +9, +11, +13, +15, +17, +19.

6 1,135 and 1,012 should be swapped round. The top sequence progresses: −52, +58, etc. The bottom sequence progresses: −70, +75, etc.

7 28 and 23 should be swapped round. The top sequence progresses: ×2 +1 at each stage. The bottom sequence progresses: ×3 −2 at each stage.

8 108 and 102 should be swapped round. The top sequence progresses: +17 at each stage. The bottom sequence progresses: +18 at each stage.

9 47 and 45 should be swapped round. The top sequence progresses: +2, +4, +6, +8, +10, +12. The bottom sequence progresses: +3, +5, +7, +9, +11, +13.

10 53 and 59 should be swapped round. The top sequence progresses: ×2, +1, ×2, +2, ×2, +3. The bottom sequence progresses: ×2, −1, ×2, −2, ×2, −3.

Assessment

Award yourself 1 point for each correct answer.

9–10	Excellent
7–8	Very good
5–6	Good
4	Average
2–3	Below average
0–1	Weak

Ten number puzzles

1 What number should replace the question mark to continue the sequence?

16, 49, 169, 256, ?

Answer

2 Exchange the position of two numbers in the equation below in order for it to be mathematically correct.

$76 \times 2^2 = 652 \div 3$

Answer

3 Five timepieces are all showing different times, 10.44, 11.06, 10.37, 10.53 and 11.05. Only one of these timepieces is showing the correct time, the remaining timepieces being 9 minutes slow, 16 minutes slow, 13 minutes fast and 12 minutes fast. What is the correct time?

Answer

4 What number should replace the question mark?

4	9	12
6	2	4
12	2	?

Answer

5 What number should replace the question mark?

1	2	3	4	6
9	7	■	3	4

7	4	?	9	8
4	8	■	2	6

Answer

6 Which number in the right-hand column is the odd one out?

3648	8794
1864	5926
2963	7296
4397	6578
1737	3728
	3474

Answer

7 What number should replace the question mark?
239 : 5470 : 572
863 : 14448 : 426
524 : ? : 726

Answer

8 What number should replace the question marks?
           3792 is to 55
and   2995 is to 66
therefore 6783 is to ??

Answer

9 What number should replace the question mark?

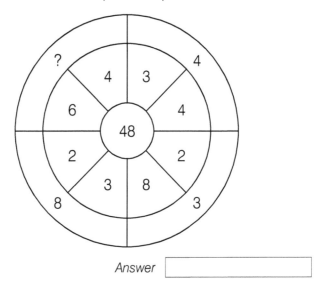

Answer [   ]

10 Mo has twice as many as Flo, and Flo has twice as many as Jo. In total they have 203. How many each have Mo, Flo and Jo?

Answer [   ]

Answers

1 169. Total up the digits of each number and then square the result. Thus, $1 + 6 = 7$ and $7 \times 7 = 49$; $4 + 9 = 13$ and $13 \times 13 = 169$; $1 + 6 + 9 = 16$ and $16 \times 16 = 256$.

2 $56 \times 2^2 = 672 \div 3$

3 10.53 is the correct time. 11.05 = 12 minutes fast, 10.37 = 16 minutes slow, 11.06 = 13 minutes fast and 10.44 = 9 minutes slow. Some readers may have spotted that, as two of the times are slow and two are fast, the correct time must be the middle one, ie 10.53.

4 8:

$4 \times 9 = 36$; $36 \div 3 = 12$

$6 \times 2 = 12$; $12 \div 3 = 4$

$12 \times 2 = 24$; $24 \div 3 = 8$

5   2: 7 + 2 = 9, 4 × 2 = 8, 4 ÷ 2 = 2 and 8 − 2 = 6, thus following the pattern of the first set of numbers.

6   6578. Each of the other numbers in the right-hand column is double one of the numbers in the left-hand column.

7   4084. The centre number in each row is the product of the digits on the left followed by the product of the digits on the right. 40 = 5 × 2 × 4; 84 = 7 × 2 × 6.

8   16: 83 − 67

9   2: 6 × 4 × 2 = 48, thus following the pattern of the numbers in the other three quadrants.

10   Mo = 116, Flo = 58, Jo = 29

Verbal ability

L ife today is all about communicating properly, and to do this effectively we need to endeavour to increase our level of verbal expertise and dexterity.

Verbal aptitude tests are widely used in intelligence (IQ) testing and typically include spelling, grammar, word meanings, completing sentences, synonyms and antonyms. Verbal aptitude is, therefore, a measurement of your capacity to use language in order to express yourself, comprehend written text and understand other people.

The puzzles and tests in this section are designed to give your brain a fun yet often challenging and thorough workout in a wide variety of exercises.

Nine-letter word search exercise

Example
Start at one of the corner squares and spiral clockwise around the perimeter, finishing at the centre square to spell out a nine-letter word. You have to provide the missing letters.

		R
A	H	I
L		N

The answer is LABYRINTH, which starts at the bottom left-hand corner square, spirals clockwise around the perimeter and finishes at the central letter, H. The missing letters are B, Y and T, and no other solution in the English language is possible.

Target time: 45 minutes.

1

O	R	R
T		A
	N	

2

N	G	E
	L	N
C	A	

3

E		O
E	M	S
T	S	

4

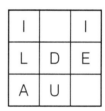

I		I
L	D	E
A	U	

5

A	U	A
N	T	
O	R	T

6

T	E	R
A	D	S
	E	

7

E	R	A
		D
S	E	D

9

N	A	
	L	R
E	T	A

8

	I	S
G	E	
A	N	A

10

	O	M
C		P
A	N	A

Answers

1   RAINSTORM
2   CONGENIAL
3   ECOSYSTEM
4   QUALIFIED
5   ASTRONAUT
6   WATERSHED
7   DESPERADO
8   MISMANAGE
9   FRATERNAL
10   ACCOMPANY

The A–Z of word building

Each of the words below can be completed by inserting the same letter several times. The number of letters to be inserted is given, but you have to work out which set of letters, from A to Z, need inserting.

For example: I N E R M I E N + 4 means the same letter needs inserting four times in order to complete the word. Apart from the four missing letters, the remaining letters given are always in the correct order.

In this case the answer is I N E R M I E N + T T T T = INTERMITTENT

The following is a list of the number of letters that need to be inserted into each word.
AAAA, BBB, CCC, DDDD, EEEE, FFF, GGGG, HHH, IIII, JJ, KK, LLLL, MMM, NNNN, OOOO, PPP, QQ, RRRR, SSSS, TTTT, UUU, VV, WWW, XX, YYY, ZZZZ.
Tick them off one by one as you complete the words below, which are not in the same alphabetical order as the letters to be inserted.

1   S N O N M + 3   *Answer* [   ]

2   D F R N C + 4   *Answer* [   ]

3   E F I G E A T O + 4   *Answer* [   ]

4   U I N U E R E M E + 2   *Answer* [   ]

5   S U I N T + 3   *Answer* [   ]

6   I L I N + 4   *Answer* [   ]

7   N H B T O N + 4   *Answer* [   ]

8   I E G A Y + 4   *Answer* [   ]

9   P O O + 3   *Answer* [   ]

10   E O L E + 2   *Answer* [   ]

11   C I U A U A + 3   *Answer* [   ]

12 E E C U T R I + 2   *Answer*

13 U L E + 3   *Answer*

14 N S A L + 3   *Answer*

15 U A O U C E D + 4   *Answer*

16 C I O R + 4   *Answer*

17 U U B E + 2   *Answer*

18 R A M A T A + 4   *Answer*

19 H A I + 2   *Answer*

20 L U + 3   *Answer*

21 F L P R F + 4   *Answer*

22 S A U E E + 4   *Answer*

23 I N I U + 3   *Answer*

24 M L G M T E + 4   *Answer*

25 G R A N A Y + 4   *Answer*

26 I N E A L E + 3   *Answer*

Answers

1 S Y N O N Y M Y
2 D E F E R E N C E
3 R E F R I G E R A T O R
4 Q U I N Q U E R E M E
5 S U C C I N C T

6 GIGGLING
7 INHIBITION
8 ILLEGALLY
9 POWWOW
10 EVOLVE
11 CHIHUAHUA
12 EXECUTRIX
13 BUBBLE
14 UNUSUAL
15 UNANNOUNCED
16 SCISSORS
17 JUJUBE
18 RAZZMATAZZ
19 KHAKI
20 FLUFF
21 FOOLPROOF
22 STATUETTE
23 MINIMUM
24 AMALGAMATE
25 GRANDDADDY
26 PINEAPPLE

Commonly confused words exercise

The answer to each question in this exercise is two words that are very similar in spelling and/or pronunciation and are often confused or misused in correspondence and conversation. Examples of such words are affect/effect, quiet/quite, envelop/envelope and alternate/alternative. You should rewrite each sentence using the two similar words that are being defined.

Example
The person granted the authority to organize proceedings could be quite meddlesome at times.

Answer   The official could be quite officious at times

1 The various types of apparel were made of different types of fabric.

Answer [   ]

2 The helpers were quick to render aid.

Answer [   ]

3 She blushed when in his company as he handed her the gifts.

Answer [   ]

4 The moisture falling in drops from the clouds splashed against the narrow strip used to guide the horse.

Answer [   ]

5 Although only existing in fancy, its creation involved a high degree of creative thought.

Answer [   ]

6 Although you may only express, or state, indirectly what may be the truth, I may then correctly deduce or conclude what the true facts are.

Answer [   ]

7 The well-bred, stylish man was extremely mild and quiet in nature.

Answer [   ]

8 Some are inclined to show off their talents, while others may show contempt for the law.

Answer [   ]

9 I would like to draw out the truth pertaining to this unlawful activity.

Answer [   ]

10 There was an exchange of mail between the letter writers.

Answer [   ]

11 He had a two-purpose role, one of which was to officiate in a combat between two people.

Answer [   ]

12 He was standing quite still holding a box of writing materials.

Answer [   ]

13 The head of the school was eager to establish the fundamental truth.

Answer [   ]

14 Although the consequences could be described as very small or unimportant, it was, nevertheless, extremely careless.

Answer [   ]

15 Although lasting for only a very brief period, it proved to be an occasion of immense importance.

Answer [   ]

16 He was a person of high honourable standing, with a great spirit of fortitude and endurance.

Answer [   ]

17 Although he is fit and qualified to be chosen for the post, his writing is incapable of being read.

Answer [   ]

18 The village fete was at one time a twice-yearly event, but it is now held every two years.

Answer [   ]

19   Some people may be free from bias or involvement, while others are completely lacking in concern.

Answer [   ]

20   He is capable of thinking and reasoning to a high degree and also capable of being understood or comprehended.

Answer [   ]

Answers

1   The **clothes** were made of different **cloths**.

2   The **assistants** were quick to render **assistance**.

3   She blushed when in his **presence** as he handed her the **presents**.

4   The **rain** splashed against the **rein**.

5   Although only **imaginary**, its creation involved a high degree of **imagination**.

6   Although you may only **imply** what may be the truth, I may then correctly **infer** what the true facts are.

7   The **genteel** man was extremely **gentle** in nature.

8   Some are inclined to **flaunt** their talents, while others may **flout** the law.

9   I would like to **elicit** the truth pertaining to this **illicit** activity.

10   There was **correspondence** between the **correspondents**.

11   He had a **dual** role, one of which was to officiate in a **duel**.

12   He was **stationary** holding a box of **stationery**.

13   The **principal** was eager to establish the **principle**.

14   Although the consequences could be described as **negligible**, it was, nevertheless, **negligent**.

15   Although **momentary**, it proved to be an occasion of **momentous** importance.

16   He was a person of high **moral** standing, with a great **morale**.

17   Although he is **eligible** for the post, his writing is **illegible**.

18   The village fete was at one time a **biannual** event, but it is now **biennial**.

19   Some people may be **disinterested**, while others are completely **uninterested**.

20   He is **intelligent** and also **intelligible**.

Cryptograms

I N THE FOLLOWING CRYPTOGRAMS EACH LETTER OF THE ALPHABET
EP XFZ MKSSKTEPO BYGCXKOYJAU ZJBF SZXXZY KM XFZ JSCFJRZX

HAS BEEN RANDOMLY REPLACED BY ANOTHER.
FJU RZZP YJPHKASG YZCSJBZH RG JPKXFZY.

A	B	C	D	E	F	G	H	I	J	K	L	M
J	R	B	H	Z	M	O	F	E	W	N	S	A
N	O	P	Q	R	S	T	U	V	W	X	Y	Z
P	K	C	V	Y	U	X	Q	I	T	L	G	D

What is commonly referred to in cryptology as a simple cryptogram is when every letter of the alphabet from A to Z (known as the plain text) is substituted for another in the coded text. For example, the letter A might be substituted by the letter J and the letter B might be substituted by the letter R, as in the example above.

   Cryptanalysts have at their disposal a great deal of information, such as letter and word frequency. The latest information on the order in which letters appear most frequently in the English language is ETAOINSHR, and the full list of the 26 letters of the alphabet together with their associated percentages is as follows:

a	8.2	n	6.7
b	1.5	o	7.5
c	2.8	p	1.9
d	4.3	q	0.1
e	12.7	r	6.0
f	2.2	s	6.3
g	2.0	t	9.1
h	6.1	u	2.5
i	7.0	v	1.0
j	0.2	w	2.4
k	0.8	x	0.2
l	4.0	y	2.0
m	2.4	z	0.1

The order in which letters appear most often at the beginning of a word is TAOSTWHCB and at the end ESDTNRYO. The most common two-letter word in the English language is OF, the most common three-letter ending in the English language is ING, and the most common double letters are EE, FF, LL, OO, RR and SS.

When solving cryptograms, always try to identify what might be the word THE, which appears in almost every paragraph in the English language, often several times, as well as looking for frequently paired letter combinations and sets of three letters. There are tables of frequencies of pairs of letters (known as digraphs) and sets of three letters (trigraphs) to assist the cryptanalyst. The 30 most common digraphs in the English language are, in order of occurrence: th, er, on, an, re, he, in, ed, nd, ha, at, en, es, of, or, nt, ea, ti, to, it, st, io, le, is, ou, ar, as, de, rt, ve. The 15 most common trigraphs are: the, and, tha, ent, ion, tio, for, nde, has, nce, edt, tis, oft, sth, men. Also look for short words, the most frequent being, in descending order: THE, OF, AND, TO, IN, THAT and IS.

1

HRUHOO SP SUUKOTSP TO HRWTYKLKGTPA. TG

QLHNHPGO BSXHLKGTSP ZLSB KUIJTLTPA GWH

XHKXHPTPA HZZHUG SZ K WKETG.

C. OSBHLOHG BKJAWKB

A	B	C	D	E	F	G	H	I	J	K	L	M

N	O	P	Q	R	S	T	U	V	W	X	Y	Z

Answer

2

TMXB MH ANB CMKOR'T VKBLABTA HBLAT CBKB

LYYMXFOUTNBR   EJ   FBMFOB   QMA   TXLKA

BQMPVN AM SQMC ANBJ CBKB UXFMTTUEOB.

RMPV OLKTMQ

A	B	C	D	E	F	G	H	I	J	K	L	M

N	O	P	Q	R	S	T	U	V	W	X	Y	Z

Answer

3

IWM XSSZ DIW DPQCQDQGL, DSWOLFW, IWO

DSFEZIQW – IWO FSYC XSSZY OS.

OIZL DIPWLJQL

A	B	C	D	E	F	G	H	I	J	K	L	M

N	O	P	Q	R	S	T	U	V	W	X	Y	Z

Answer [   ]

4

UVNTCZATZE'L NQTI VM EGT TBVZVAO BVYPW

FT LYAATW YD QZ J MTI LGVCE DGCJLTL: QM QE

AVNTL EJR QE, QM QE XTTDL AVNQZU CTUYPJET

QE, JZW QM QE LEVDL AVNQZU LYFLQWQKT QE.

CVZJPW CTJUJZ

A	B	C	D	E	F	G	H	I	J	K	L	M

N	O	P	Q	R	S	T	U	V	W	X	Y	Z

Answer [   ]

5

RDK AIUX LKALUK ODA ZJIB ODNR RDKX NQK

UAAGJIY ZAQ JI UJZK NQK RDK ZNMUR

ZJIBKQC.

ZACRKQ'C UNO

A	B	C	D	E	F	G	H	I	J	K	L	M
N	O	P	Q	R	S	T	U	V	W	X	Y	Z

Answer [   ]

6

CQEQNEWJ WC ZTMNM ITM GMXMVDHMN

EQVVGDRMC DQI ITM INMMC, ITMK KJAMC ITM

CINMMIC JPIMN ITMA.

EWVV XJQBTK

A	B	C	D	E	F	G	H	I	J	K	L	M
N	O	P	Q	R	S	T	U	V	W	X	Y	Z

Answer [   ]

Answers

1   Excess on occasion is exhilarating. It prevents moderation
     from acquiring the deadening effect of a habit.
     W. Somerset Maugham ·

2   Some of the world's greatest feats were accomplished by
     people not smart enough to know they were impossible.
     Doug Larson

3   Any fool can criticize, condemn, and complain – and most
     fools do.
     Dale Carnegie

4   Government's view of the economy could be summed up in a
     few short phrases: if it moves tax it, if it keeps moving regulate
     it, and if it stops moving subsidize it.
     Ronald Reagan

5   The only people who find what they are looking for in life are
     the fault finders.
     Foster's Law

6   Suburbia is where the developer bulldozes out the trees, then
     names the streets after them.
     Bill Vaughn

Locate the countries

In each of the 25 questions in this puzzle it is necessary to find the
name of a country with the help of the two clues provided. Each of
the clues leads to a one-word answer, the number of letters in the
answer being indicated. The first few letters of the first answer are
the first few letters of a country and the final few letters of the second
answer are the final few letters of that same country. The number of
letters in the name of each country is also indicated.

For example:
Spitefulness (6)
An elaborate celebratory festival (6)
Country (5)

Answer:
malice
fies**ta**
Country: Malta

1 Branch of mathematics (7)
Standards of judging or established rules (8)
Country (7)

Answer [   ]

2 Small burrowing rodent, sometimes kept as a pet (6)
The language of the gypsies (6)
Country (7)

Answer [   ]

3 The Roman god of love (5)
Percussion instrument with wooden bars similar to a xylo-
phone (7)
Country (4)

Answer [   ]

4 Nerve cell (6)
Any of eight small bones of the wrist (6)
Country (5)

Answer [   ]

5 A painting of a person's face (8)
Avoiding waste (6)
Country (8)

Answer [   ]

6 An intuition (5)
Sweet (6)
Country (7)

Answer [   ]

7   Dog house (6)
Spicy Creole dish (9)
Country (5)

Answer [   ]

8   To go out (6)
Cellar or vault beneath a church (5)
Country (5)

Answer [   ]

9   The words of an opera (8)
Delirium or frenzy (8)
Country (7)

Answer [   ]

10   To leap and frisk about in play (4)
An intense love for yourself and your own needs (8)
Country (7)

Answer [   ]

11   Set in from the margin (6)
A dark brown colour (5)
Country (5)

Answer [   ]

12   Courteous (6)
Spread out (6)
Country (6)

Answer [   ]

13   Specialized technical terminology (6)
Almond paste and egg white (8)
Country (5)

Answer [   ]

14 Painting on wet plaster on a wall (6)
A meeting of spiritualists (6)
Country (6)

Answer

15 Large in size or number (5)
Female relative (5)
Country (6)

Answer

16 Maker of men's garments (6)
Graceful aquatic bird (4)
Country (6)

Answer

17 Freedom from imprisonment (7)
Large oval melon-like fruit with yellowish flesh (6)
Country (5)

Answer

18 List individually (7)
Deviation from the normal rule (7)
Country (5)

Answer

19 Impudent (6)
Dock for yachts and cabin cruisers (6)
Country (5)

Answer

20 Annul (6)
Fleet of ships (6)
Country (6)

Answer

21 Selection (6)
Meek (6)
Country (5)

Answer [   ]

22 An arachnid (6)
Get (6)
Country (5)

Answer [   ]

23 Violent agitation (7)
Horse race rider (6)
Country (6)

Answer [   ]

24 Unsightly (4)
Black and white herbivorous mammal (5)
Country (6)

Answer [   ]

25 Cardigan or pullover (7)
Aureate (6)
Country (6)

Answer [   ]

Answers

1 algebra, criteria – Algeria
2 gerbil, Romany – Germany
3 Cupid, marimba – Cuba
4 neuron, carpal – Nepal
5 portrait, frugal – Portugal
6 hunch, sugary – Hungary
7 kennel, jambalaya – Kenya
8 egress, crypt – Egypt

9 libretto, hysteria – Liberia
10 romp, egomania – Romania
11 indent, sepia – India
12 polite, expand – Poland
13 jargon, marzipan – Japan
14 fresco, seance – France
15 great, niece – Greece
16 tailor, swan – Taiwan
17 liberty, papaya – Libya
18 itemize, anomaly – Italy
19 cheeky, marina – China
20 cancel, armada – Canada
21 choice, docile – Chile
22 spider, obtain – Spain
23 turmoil, jockey – Turkey
24 ugly, panda – Uganda
25 sweater, golden – Sweden

Ten word puzzles

1 What word can be placed in the brackets so that it produces new words or phrases when placed behind all the words on the left and new words or phrases when placed in front of all the words on the right?

Bare			log
Cut			drop
Out	(	)	hand
Call			bite
Hard			space

Answer [ ]

2 In all of the following change one letter only in each word below to form a familiar phrase. For example:
lust bat now leapt = last but not least

i   an tie was cut

Answer

ii   feat but

Answer

iii   torch any so

Answer

iv   to of pie

Answer

v   ere no ewe

Answer

vi   end to of

Answer

vii   none so tall

Answer

viii   race go fame

Answer

ix   so bells us

Answer

x   skate if toe are

Answer

xi   line i wish but on waver

Answer

xii   get thee sat cane

Answer

xiii   toe did as cart

Answer

xiv now in tour line

Answer

xv don on i run

Answer

xvi us is she sir

Answer

3 The answer to each clue is a one-word answer that always contains the word FUN, either at the beginning or somewhere in the middle, but not at the end, as there is no word in the English language ending in FUN. For example:

No longer in force or use (7)

Answer | defunct

i Intellectual depth, penetrating knowledge, keen insight, etc (10)

Answer

ii A failing to work correctly (11)

Answer

iii A railway up the side of a mountain (9)

Answer

iv A conical shape with a wider and narrower opening at the two ends (6)

Answer

v To reimburse (6)

Answer

vi A formal or social gathering (8)

Answer

vii A parasitic plant such as mildew (6)

Answer

viii Basic, essential (11)

        Answer [   ]

ix Humourless (7)

        Answer [   ]

4 Arrange the letters in the grid to produce a magic word square where the same four 4-letter words can be read both across and down.

A	C	E	E
E	H	H	J
M	M	O	S
O	S	T	T

Answer

5 Find the starting point and work from letter to adjacent letter horizontally and vertically, but not diagonally, to spell out a 12-letter word. You must provide the missing letters.

L	A	N	R
A	T	S	
R		U	P

Answer [   ]

6 Insert a word for a type of geographical feature into the bottom row to produce nine 3-letter words reading downwards.

D	T	P	F	M	O	S	N	O
E	E	I	O	A	A	E	I	W

7 Place the names of two types of horse on the first and fourth rows to produce eight 4-letter words reading downwards.

E	U	B	I	U	D	M	E
A	S	L	L	L	E	E	E

8 Place two 'this and that' words into each set of letters to produce two words in each puzzle. For example:
C E E and F R T
Answer
Add OFF and ON to the two sets of letters to produce COFFEE and FRONT.

    i A N E D and A A B L E (clue: invalid)

              Answer [   ]

    ii B E T and A C C G (clue: destruction)

              Answer [   ]

    iii F L Y and D E D (clue: general membership)

              Answer [   ]

    iv E N T D and T I S S (clue: entertain)

              Answer [   ]

v   A N E and A F N T (clue: fluctuate)

Answer [   ]

vi   E R T and L A N E R (clue: alternating)

Answer [   ]

9   Complete the seven types of vegetable below. Only alternate letters are shown. Then rearrange the initial letters of each of the seven vegetables to produce an eighth vegetable.

* E * T * O * T

Answer [   ]

* S * A * A * U *

Answer [   ]

* H * R * I *

Answer [   ]

* R * S *

Answer [   ]

* G * P * A * T

Answer [   ]

* R * C * O * I

Answer [   ]

* R * I * H * K *

Answer [   ]

Anagram [   ]

10   Magic word square

The answers to the clues are all five-letter words that, when placed correctly into the grid, will form a magic word square where the same five words can be read both horizontally and vertically.

The clues are in no particular order:

- radio detection and ranging

- sleepy

- the least suitable

- giraffe-like animal

- that which is surplus to immediate requirements

Answers

1 back

2
  i on the way out
  ii flat out
  iii touch and go
  iv do or die
  v eye to eye
  vi and so on
  vii nose to tail
  viii face to face
  ix go belly up
  x state of the art
  xi like a fish out of water
  xii let them eat cake
  xiii the die is cast

VERBAL ABILITY **85**

xiv not on your life
xv son of a gun
xvi up in the air
3 **i** profundity
ii malfunction
iii funicular
iv funnel
v refund
vi function
vii fungus
viii fundamental
ix unfunny

4

J	E	S	T
E	C	H	O
S	H	A	M
T	O	M	E

5 SUPERNATURAL
6 WATERFALL: DEW, TEA, PIT, FOE, MAR, OAF, SEA, NIL, OWL
7 STALLION and SHETLAND: SEAS, TUSH, ABLE, LILT, LULL, IDEA, OMEN, NEED
8 **i** A N**NULL**E D and A **VOID** A B L E
ii B **RACK**E T and A C C **RUIN** G
iii F **RANK**L Y and D E **FILE** D
iv E N T**WINE**D and T I **DINE**S S
v A **TO**N E and A F **FRO**N T
vi E R **UP**T and L A N **DOWN**E R
9 beetroot, asparagus, gherkin, cress, eggplant, broccoli, artichoke
Anagram: cabbage

10

W	O	R	S	T
O	K	A	P	I
R	A	D	A	R
S	P	A	R	E
T	I	R	E	D

CHAPTER 5

Sharpen up your memory

Memory is the process of storing and retrieving information in the brain. It is this process of memory that is central to our learning and thinking.

Human beings are continually learning throughout their lifetime but only some of this massive volume of information is selected and stored by the brain, and this becomes available later for recall when required. Learning is the acquisition of new knowledge, and memory is the retention of this knowledge. This powerful combination of learning and memory is, therefore, the basis of all our knowledge and abilities. It is what enables us to consider the past, exist in the present and plan for the future. While little is known about the physiology of memory storage in the brain, what is known is that memory is not situated in just one part of the brain but involves the association of several brain systems working together.

There are certain techniques by which we are all able to improve our memory, and it is accepted that the more you use it the better it becomes. It is, therefore, important to stimulate the memory by using it to the utmost and learning new skills. In addition to enriching our lives, this could also stimulate our brain's neural circuits to grow and strengthen.

The tests that follow are designed to assist you in improving your memory by developing your powers of concentration, and to discipline yourself on the subject under examination.

Ten memory puzzles

1 A _____

    B _____

    C _____

    D _____

    E _____

Study the above for 10 seconds and then turn straight to page 90.

Questions

i Which is the longest line?

Answer [   ]

ii Which is the shortest line?

Answer [   ]

2   Study and memorize this paragraph for 1 minute; then turn immediately to page 92 and answer the question that you will find there.

Question

How many times does the letter r appear in the paragraph?

Answer

3

→	↓
↓	←

Study the above for 10 seconds; then wait for 1 minute before turning to page 94.

Question

Which one of the following did you look at 1 minute ago?

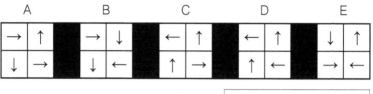

Answer

⁴ **M E** *M* **O R Y**

Study the above for 30 seconds and then turn straight to page 96.

Question

Which one of the following have you just looked at?

A	**M**	**E**	M	O	**R**	**Y**
B	**M**	E	*M*	O	R	**Y**
C	**M**	**E**	**M**	O	**R**	**Y**
D	**M**	**E**	*M*	O	R	**Y**
E	**M**	E	**M**	**O**	**R**	Y

Answer [   ]

5 This exercise tests your ability to remember names and form
associations.

SUZANNE	MATTHEW	HEATHER
RAYMOND	EUGENIE	ANDY
CAROL	GABRIELLE	JONATHAN
VINCENT	JAMIE	STEPHANIE
LISA	STUART	JAKE
ROBERT	CAROLINE	DOROTHY

Study the nine pairs of names for 3 minutes and use your imagination to link each pair of names, as shown above. Now turn to
page 98.

Question

Put a letter A against one pair, the letter B against a second pair, and so on, through to the letter I, until you have matched what you think are the original nine pairs of names.

ROBERT   _____

ANDY   _____

GABRIELLE   _____

JONATHAN   _____

SUZANNE   _____

VINCENT   _____

LISA   _____

CAROLINE   _____

DOROTHY   _____

JAMIE   _____

RAYMOND   _____

JAKE   _____

CAROL   _____

MATTHEW   _____

STEPHANIE   _____

STUART   _____

HEATHER   _____

EUGENIE   _____

6

Study the above grid for 1 minute; then turn straight to page 100.

Questions

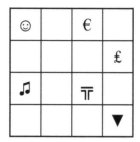

i Which two symbols have changed places?

Answer [   ]

ii Which new symbol has been introduced?

Answer [   ]

iii Which symbol has been removed?

Answer [   ]

7 This exercise tests your ability to remember pairs of words and form associations.

CAMERA	CANDLE	MAGNIFYING GLASS
LEMON	IPOD	PEANUT
CABBAGE	TEAPOT	TRAMPOLINE
MOUSE	CHAIR	SKATEBOARD
COMB	COCONUT	TELEPHONE
BOOK	SAND	HAMSTER
PIANO	BROOCH	SEAGULL
CANOE	HOTEL	REFRIGERATOR

Study the 12 pairs of words for 10 minutes and use your imagination to link each pair of words in as many ways as possible. Now turn to page 102.

Question

Put a letter A against one pair, the letter B against a second pair, and so on, through to the letter L, until you have matched what you think are the original 12 pairs of words.

SKATEBOARD

COCONUT

CAMERA

BOOK

SEAGULL

PIANO

MOUSE

PEANUT

LEMON

MAGNIFYING GLASS

TELEPHONE

CANDLE

COMB

REFRIGERATOR

CABBAGE

BROOCH

CANOE

CHAIR

TRAMPOLINE

IPOD

TEAPOT

HOTEL

HAMSTER

SAND

8   Study the set of figures below for 1 minute; then turn straight
to page 104.

Question

Which pair of figures below appears in the same order twice?

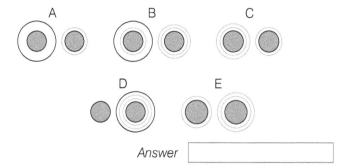

Answer

9 Study the two figures below for 30 seconds; then wait for 1 minute before turning to page 106.

Question

Which two figures did you look at 1 minute ago?

A   B   C   D   E

Answer

10   Study the set of figures below for 2 minutes; then turn straight
to page 108.

♪ ▶ 9 $ 4 Ω 3 ♠ 9 ♫ W 7 $ &

Questions

i   Which symbol appears in the set twice?

Answer [   ]

ii   Which number appears in the set twice?

Answer [   ]

iii   What number appears immediately before the spade ♠?

Answer [   ]

iv   What letter appears immediately before the number 7?

Answer [   ]

CHAPTER 6

Brain-teaser puzzles

B esides recreational value, one of the major benefits to be derived from tackling puzzles is that they stretch and exercise the mind and involve different and, sometimes, original and creative thought processes. The 12 puzzles in this chapter have been devised with exactly that in mind, and they provide a varied challenge in terms of both content and level of difficulty.

Twelve brain-teaser puzzles

1 Find the starting point and read clockwise to spell out a familiar phrase. Only alternate letters are shown.

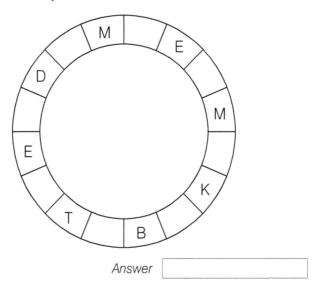

Answer _____

2 What letter should replace the question mark?

P	A	T	H	T	D
M	O	S	A	E	?

Answer _____

3 Complete the following to find five names all on the same theme, each five letters long.

Y * * * *

Answer _____

* Y * * *

Answer _____

* * Y * *

Answer [   ]

* * * Y *

Answer [   ]

* * * * Y

Answer [   ]

4 What is the largest number that, when spelled out in the English language (for example 60 = sixty), does not repeat any letters?

Answer [   ]

5 An electrical circuit wiring a set of four lights depends on a system of switches A, B, C and D. Each switch when working has the following effect on the lights:

Switch A turns lights 1 and 2 on/off or off/on.
Switch B turns lights 2 and 4 on/off or off/on.
Switch C turns lights 1 and 3 on/off or off/on.
Switch D turns lights 3 and 4 on/off or off/on.

[⬤] = ON

[ ] = OFF

In the following, switches C A D B are thrown in turn, with the result that Figure 1 is transformed into Figure 2. One of the switches is not, therefore, working and has had no effect on the numbered lights. Identify which one of the switches is not working.

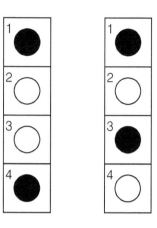

Answer [   ]

6   Complete the grid so that every straight line across and down contains one each of:
X, Y, Z, 4, 5.

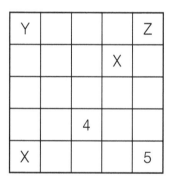

7   If meat in a river (3 in 6) is T(ham)es, can you find the containers in each of the following 11 puzzles:

   i   The pinnacle in a state of ideal perfection (3 in 6)

            Answer [   ]

  ii   Kitchen appliance in a written agreement (4 in 8)

            Answer [   ]

iii A boar in a large tree valued for its wood (3 in 8)

Answer [   ]

iv Shakespeare title character in permission to proceed (4 in 9)

Answer [   ]

v Fruit in an image (3 in 6)

Answer [   ]

vi Metallic element in the surrounding areas (4 in 8)

Answer [   ]

vii Swine in a pipe joint (3 in 6)

Answer [   ]

viii Sailing vessel in a hat shop (5 in 9)

Answer [   ]

ix Taxi in a sheath (3 in 8)

Answer [   ]

x Asian country in a crafty and involved plot (5 in 11)

Answer [   ]

xi US president in a Russian peasant woman's headscarf (4 in 8)

Answer [   ]

8 Find the starting point and work from letter to adjacent letter horizontally, vertically and diagonally to spell out a phrase. Every letter is used once each only.

I	O	N		T	I	S
T	I	F		C	S	T
C	N	F	A	G	A	R
		A	E	N		
	H	T	R			

Answer

9 Find the starting point and work from letter to adjacent letter horizontally, vertically and diagonally to spell a three-word description of commonly seen devices. Every letter is used once each only.

		S		
	T	I	N	
P	L	A	Y	U	V
S	I	D	U	S	I
	L	A		

Answer

10 Which number is the odd one out?

34847   72423   65602   46944   42729   53755   47843

Answer

11 erbium, ?, coerce, expert, answer
Which word is missing?
cherry, aerial, oyster, unable, trendy

Answer

12 In this crossword each clue is an anagram of the word you are
seeking to fit in the crossword.

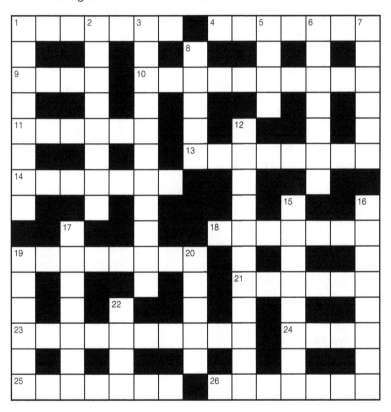

Clues:

ACROSS
1 go nurse (7)
4 tail cap (7)
9 bare (4)
10 nettle stem (10)
11 air lad (6)
13 base toga (8)
14 or sauce (7)
18 stun lie (7)
19 it dances (8)
21 decree(6)
23 estimating (10)
24 cone (4)
25 cane hen (7)
26 ran deal (7)

DOWN
1 bust cart (8)
2 sing roar (8)
3 select boson (11)
5 ripe (4)
6 let harm (7)
7 tell it (6)
8 a salt (5)
12 table editor (11)
15 eaten cod (8)
16 Elbe bull (8)
17 to Chris (7)
19 led tee (6)
20 pique (5)
22 name (4)

Answers

1 make both ends meet
2 O. Start at M and move from bottom to top alternately to spell MASHED. Start at P and move from top to bottom alternately to spell POTATO.
3 Yemen, Syria, Egypt, Libya, Italy
4 five thousand
5 Switch D is faulty.
6

Y	4	X	5	Z
Z	5	Y	X	4
4	Z	5	Y	X
5	X	4	Z	Y
X	Y	Z	4	5

7   **i**   U(top)ia   **vii**   s(pig)ot
    ii   c(oven)ant   **viii**   mil(liner)y
    iii ma(hog)any   **ix**   s(cab)bard
    iv   c(lear)ance   **x**   ma(china)tion
    v   ef(fig)y   **xi**   ba(bush)ka
    vi   env(iron)s

8   fact is stranger than fiction

9   visual display units

10   46944: in all the others the first, second and last digits multiplied together equal the number formed by the remaining two digits, for example 34847: $3 \times 4 \times 7 = 84$

11   aerial: the letters er are moving up one place each time

12

¹S	U	²R	G	E	³O	N		⁴C	⁵A	P	⁶I	T	A	⁷L
U		A		B		⁸A			I		H			I
⁹B	E	A	R		¹⁰S	E	T	T	L	E	M	E	N	T
T		R		O		L		R		R				T
¹¹R	A	D	I	A	L		A		¹²O			M		L
A		S		E		¹³S	A	B	O	T	A	G	E	
¹⁴C	A	R	O	U	S	E		L			L			
T		N		C				I		¹⁵A			¹⁶B	
	¹⁷O		E		¹⁸U	T	E	N	S	I	L			
¹⁹D	I	S	T	A	N	C	²⁰E		E		E			U
E		T		T		Q		²¹R	E	C	E	D	E	
L		R	²²A		U		A		D				B	
²³E	N	I	G	M	A	T	I	S	T		²⁴O	N	C	E
T		C		E		P		E		T			L	
²⁵E	N	H	A	N	C	E		²⁶A	D	R	E	N	A	L

CHAPTER 7

3D thinking

Next, when you are describing
A shape, or sound, or tint;
Don't state the matter plainly,
But put it in a hint;
And learn to look at all things,
With a sort of mental squint.

Lewis Carroll

The advantages of 3D thinking, or creative or lateral thinking as it is
sometimes referred to, are considerable. Instead of looking merely
at what is on the surface of any problem, we are able to look beyond
what might on first inspection be apparent and thus find solutions
to puzzles or real-life problems that may not seem evident on first
inspection. By developing this type of thinking we are able to view
things from many different perspectives.

To solve the 15 puzzles in this chapter it is necessary to think
laterally and creatively and, in many cases, look for solutions that
may not seem apparent on first inspection.

Fifteen 3D thinking puzzles

1 Which two words (one from each column) are in the wrong column?

hijacked	turn
facile	sporty
pours	blamed
calmed	rosy
behalf	sprout
fabled	town
medical	rusty
flicked	you
lamb	snout
gamble	upturn

Answer [   ]

2 What number should replace the question mark?

93	48	6	71	25
76	29	58	1	34
28	17	54	39	6
81	79	26	3	45
?	91	47	63	28

Answer [   ]

3

?

Which figure should replace the question mark?

| A | B | C | D | E |

Answer [   ]

4 Which two numbers come next?
14, 5, 19, 10, 29, 11, 40, ?, ?

Answer [   ]

5 What letter should replace the question mark?

Answer [   ]

6 If J = 167 and M = 35, what does N equal?

Answer [   ]

7 In which column should the word WRY be placed?

TO	FLASH
OPT	SAG
POT	LADS

Answer [   ]

8 The arrangement of letters S I O U T D E leads to which familiar phrase?

Answer _____

9 How much soil does a round hole contain that measures 5 feet in diameter and is 16 feet deep?

Answer _____

10 A reader places a bookmark in a book. It is either between pages 73 and 74, 159 and 160 or 128 and 129. Between which two pages is the bookmark?

Answer _____

11 The arrangement of letters below leads to which familiar phrase?

```
                              E
                              S
                              R
T        H        E        W        O
```

Answer _____

12 Jim Clark, Tony Knowles, Lawrence Durrell
Who below makes up a foursome?
A   Vyacheslav Mikhailovich Molotov
B   1st Earl Kitchener of Khartoum
C   1st Viscount Montgomery of Alamein
D   René Antoine Ferchault de Réaumur
E   Edward George Earle Bulwer-Lytton

Answer _____

13 frowey, serif
What do the above words have in common, and which word below has the same thing in common with them?
dig, choose, smug, polish, cheese, grab

Answer _____

14 loofah, beeswax, fabric, abscond
What comes next?
cardboard, abundance, lily, pioneer, calamity

Answer _____

15 odor, trek, omit, afar, esox, plan, stir, ?
What comes next?
hemp, color, snag, idol, note, tuft, humor

Answer _____

Answers

1 pours and blamed. The first column consists of words spelled with letters from the first half of the alphabet. The second column consists of letters spelled with letters from the second half of the alphabet.

2 5: each line of numbers across contains the digits 1 to 9 once each only

3 C

The column contains the letters E I F F E L complete with mirror image.

4 4, 44

14, 1 + 4 = 5, 14 + 5 = 19, 1 + 9 = 10, 19 + 10 = 29, 2 + 9 = 11, 29 + 11 = 40, 4 + 0 = 4, 40 + 4 = 44

5 X: so that the letters inside the hexagon can be arranged to spell the word HEXAGON

6 N = 11

J = months 1, 6 and 7 – January, June and July

M = months 3 and 5 – March and May

N = month 11 – November

7 The first column consists of letters contained on the first row of a computer keyboard: QWERTYUIOP. The second column consists of letters from the second row of a computer keyboard: ASDFGHJKL.

8 inside out

9 None: a hole does not contain any soil.

10 128 and 129: the other numbers are on opposite sides of the same page

11 a turn for the worse

12 B: 1st Earl Kitchener of Khartoum: his name contains the name of a bird (1st Earl Kitc**hen**er of Khartoum), as do the other three: Jim C**lark**, Tony Kn**owl**es, La**wren**ce Durrell

13 smug: it ends with a tree in reverse, gum, as do the other two words: yew, fir

14 abundance: each word contains an additional letter of the English alphabet in turn: a, ab, abc, abcd, abcde

15 idol: the middle two letters of each word produce the diatonic scale: do, re, mi, fa, so, la, ti, do.

PART THREE

IQ test

CHAPTER 8

IQ test 2

A time limit of 120 minutes is allowed for completion of all 40 questions. The correct answers are given at the end of the test, and you should award yourself 1 point for each completely correct answer. Calculators should not be used to assist with solving numerical questions. However, written notes may be made.

1 I travel to work by bus and train. If my bus journey takes 37 minutes and my train journey takes 19 minutes longer, what is my total travelling time in hours and minutes?

Answer [   ]

2 Change two words only in the sentence below so that it then makes complete sense.
The play chronicles the respective love of teenagers Romeo and Juliet, who become victims of the bitter feud between their doomed families.

Answer [   ]

3 Start at one of the corner squares and spiral clockwise around the perimeter, finishing at the centre square to spell out a nine-letter word. You have to provide the missing letters.

O	R	S
T		I
A	N	

Answer [   ]

4   Which word in brackets is most opposite in meaning to the word in capitals?
IMPREGNABLE (unimposing, awkward, secure, vulnerable, conceivable)

Answer [   ]

5   Which two numbers come next to continue the sequence?
0, 1, 5, 4, 11, 8, 18, 13, 26, 19, ? , ?

Answer [   ]

6

Which figure is missing?

A	B	C	D	E

Answer [   ]

7   Which is the odd one out?
alliteration, conjunction, metaphor, euphemism, simile

Answer [   ]

8 In the two numerical sequences below, one number that appears in the top sequence should appear in the bottom sequence and vice versa. Which two numbers should be changed round?

2, 5, 9, 15, 20, 27, 35

3, 5, 9, 14, 23, 33, 45

Answer

9 Identify two words (one from each set of brackets) that form a connection (analogy), thereby relating to the words in capitals in the same way.

STOP (start, gap, watch, over)

SUN (moon, star, down, dial)

Answer

10 What number should replace the question mark?

2	3	5
4	5	7
5	6	?

Answer

11 Which two words are closest in meaning?

contrivance, chronicle, chart, devise, appropriate, contrive

Answer

12   How many lines appear below?

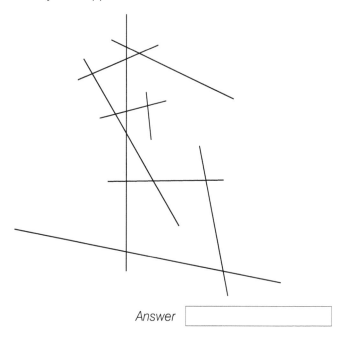

Answer [   ]

13   Identify two words (one from each set of brackets) that form a connection (analogy), thereby relating to the words in capitals in the same way.
WHOLE (amount, holistic, augury, concept)
PART (time, atomistic, community, analgesic)

Answer [   ]

14   What number should replace the question mark to continue the sequence?
40, 29.25, 18.5, 7.75, ?

Answer [   ]

15   Which two words are most opposite in meaning?
stimulate, purify, regress, downgrade, wax, please

Answer [   ]

16

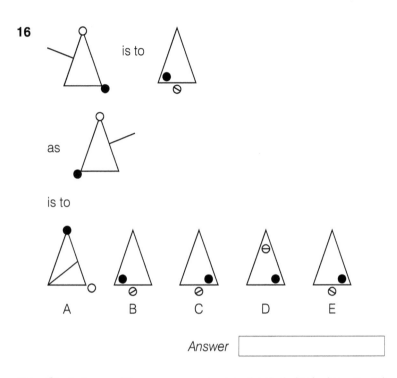

Answer [   ]

17 Start at one of the corner squares and spiral clockwise around the perimeter, finishing at the centre square to spell out a nine-letter word. You have to provide the missing letters.

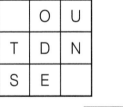

	O	U
T	D	N
S	E	

Answer [   ]

18 What is the average of all the numbers greater than 6 in the list below?

4 5 7 3 9 8 1 5 2 3 7 4 9 2 9 7 4

Answer [   ]

19   What number should replace the question mark to continue
the sequence?
100, 87, 72, 59, 44, 31, ?

Answer

20   Add five consecutive letters to the following group of letters,
and then rearrange all eight letters to produce a commonly
used word in the English language.
A C I

Answer

21

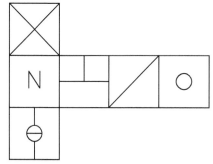

When the above is folded to form a cube, which is the only one
of the following that *cannot* be produced?

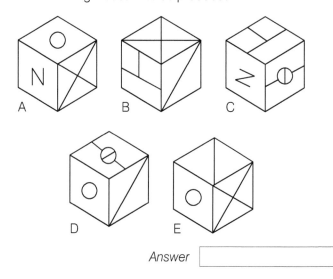

Answer

22 Which two words when combined mean ENJOYMENT?
rate, time, cart, plea, hope, lace, less, sure

Answer [   ]

23

| 3 | ? | × | 1 | 2 | = | 4 | 5 | 6 |

Which number will correctly complete the equation?

Answer [   ]

24 Select two words that are synonyms, plus an antonym of these two synonyms, from the list of words below.
attractive, belligerent, indigent, benign, reliable, candid, pugnacious

Answer [   ]

25 What number should replace the question mark?

Answer [   ]

26 How many minutes is it before 12 noon if 27 minutes ago it was twice as many minutes past 9 am?

Answer [   ]

27

is to

as

is to

A   B   C

D   E

Answer

28   In the two numerical sequences below, one number that appears in the top sequence should appear in the bottom sequence and vice versa. Which two numbers should be changed round?

1, 16, 33, 48, 65, 80, 98

2, 19, 34, 51, 66, 83, 97

Answer

29   What number is 24 less than when multiplied by seven times itself?

Answer

30   Which is the odd one out?

pelvis, scapula, clavicle, femur, dendrite

Answer

31   The ratio of men to women in an engineering factory is 7 : 2. If 882 people work in the factory, how many are men?

Answer [   ]

32

is to

as

is to

A   B   C

D   E   F

Answer [   ]

33   If Barry takes two from Harry he has twice as many as Carrie, but if instead he takes two from Carrie then Harry has twice as many as Carrie and Barry has three times more than Carrie. How many each have Carrie, Harry and Barry?

Answer [   ]

34 What number should replace the question marks?
1973 (92), 6847 (115), 3627 (??)

Answer

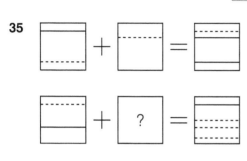

35

Which is the missing square?

A   B   C   D   E

Answer

36 What number should replace the question mark?

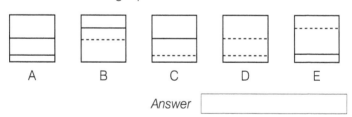

3	8	2	4
7	9	6	3
6	2	1	2
4	5	2	?

Answer

37   Which is the odd one out?

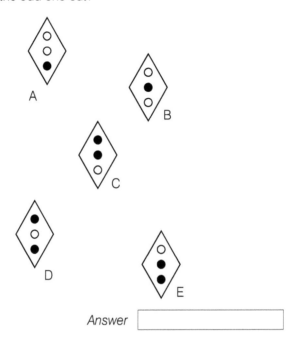

Answer [   ]

38   An electric water pump is able to pump water at a rate of 11.5 gallons per minute. How long will it take to fill up a 552-gallon tank?

Answer [   ]

39   There were 3.5 times as many telephone calls received between 12 noon and 2 pm as were received between 10 am and 12 noon. In total 216 phone calls were received between 10 am and 2 pm. How many were received between 12 noon and 2 pm?

Answer [   ]

40

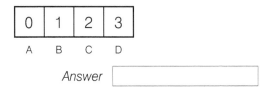

Which number will correctly complete the equation?

0	1	2	3
A	B	C	D

Answer

Answers

1   1 hour 33 minutes

2   The play chronicles the **doomed** love of teenagers Romeo and Juliet, who become victims of the bitter feud between their **respective** families.

3   signatory

4   vulnerable

5   35, 26
There are two interwoven sequences. The first, starting at 0, progresses: +5, +6 +7, +8. The second, starting at 1, progresses: +3, +4, +5, +6.

6   C: The first three figures are repeated, but only the bottom half is shown.

7   conjunction
It is a word that serves to conjoin words or phrases. The rest are figures of speech.

8   15 and 14 should be swapped round.
The top sequence progresses: +3, +4, +5, +6, +7, +8.
The bottom sequence progresses +2, +4, +6, +8, +10, +12.

9   watch and dial, to produce two types of timepiece – stopwatch and sundial

10 8
Lines across progress +1, +2. Lines down progress +2, +1.

11 devise, contrive

12 9

13 holistic, atomistic

14 −3: deduct 10.75 each time

15 regress, wax

16 C: The black dot transfers to the opposite inside bottom corner, the white dot goes to the bottom, and the line goes inside the white dot.

17 westbound

18 8

19 16: deduct 13 and 15 alternately

20 ACl + LMNOP = complain

21 A

22 pleasure

23 8

24 Synonyms: belligerent, pugnacious
Antonym: benign

25 8: $(6 \times 12) \div 9$

26 51 minutes
12 noon less 51 minutes = 11.09
11.09 less 27 minutes = 10.42
9 am plus 102 (51×2) minutes = 10.42

27 C: the whole figure rotates 90° anticlockwise

28 98 and 97 should be swapped round.
The top sequence progresses +15, +17. The bottom sequence progresses +17, +15.

29 4

30 dendrite: it is a nerve, the rest being bones

31 686
$882 \div 9$ (7 + 2) = 98
$98 \times 7 = 686$

32 D: The far left shape moves to the bottom, the second from the left moves to the middle right, the second from the right moves to the middle left, and the far right moves to the top.

33 Carrie 6, Harry 8, Barry 10

34 63: 36 + 27

35 A: Lines are carried forward from the first two squares to the final square except that they then change from full lines to broken and vice versa.

36 0

$4 \times 5 = 20$

Similarly $3 \times 8 = 24$, etc

37 E: A is the same as C with black/white dot reversal. Similarly B is the same as D.

38 48 minutes

$552 \div 11.5$

39 168

48 between 10 am and 12 noon

$48 \times 3.5 = 168$ between 12 noon and 2 pm

40 B

Assessment

Score 1 point for each correct answer.

Total score	Rating	Percentage of population
37–40	Genius level	Top 5%
32–36	High expert	Top 10%
28–31	Expert	Top 30%
24–27	High average	Top 40%
17–23	Middle average	Top 60%
13–16	Low average	Bottom 40%
9–12	Borderline low	Bottom 30%
5–8	Low	Bottom 10%
0–4	Very low	Bottom 5%

Lightning Source UK Ltd.
Milton Keynes UK
UKHW021509280121
377826UK00013B/279